Great Odd Sock Mystery

and Other Writing Prompts

Written by Melissa Gijsbers

©2023 Melissa Gijsbers
melissagijsbers.com

Finish This Book Press

Written by Melissa Gijsbers

Cover Design by Melissa Gijsbers with elements from Canva.com

ISBN: 978-0-6459968-2-1

All rights reserved. Apart from any permitted use under the Copyright Act, no part of this book may be reproduced, copied, scanned, stored in a retrieval system, recorded or transmitted in any form or by any means, without the prior permission of the publisher.

Dedication

To all the young writers that attend writers' group and encourage me to keep coming up with fun writing prompts.

Table of Contents

Dedication iii
Introduction 1
Melissa's Golden Rules of Writing 3
Tips on how to use Writing Prompts 5
Writing Prompts 6
Conclusion 58
Author Bio 59
Acknowledgements 60
Want More? 61

Introduction

Welcome writers,

Creative writing is a lot of fun, and to get started is through writing prompts. Writing prompts are designed to be a starting point for your imagination. Once you've started, you're free to let your writing take you anywhere you like!

Have fun with the prompts in this book, and try out different styles of writing—fiction, non-fiction, poetry, play, newspaper article, or something completely different.

You might like to mix things up by writing some stories in first person and others in third person. You may even want to try some poetry or a genre you haven't written before.

Remember, writing prompts don't have to be taken literally, or you may want to do just that. Use the prompts as a starting point and see where the story takes you.

By letting the story lead, you may find that these prompts head in completely unexpected directions.

When you are writing, don't worry about your first draft not being perfect. You can fix up any spelling or grammatical mistakes in your next draft. That is what editing is for.

I hope you enjoy these writing prompts.

Happy Writing!

Melissa Gijsbers

Melissa's Golden Rules of Writing

1. **Have FUN!** - creative writing is all about the process. After all, if you're not having fun, what's the point?

2. **It's YOUR Story**—write your story your way. There is no single way to write a story, so experiment, play, and write whatever comes to mind.

3. **Experiment**—play with different styles and genre. You never know what you'll enjoy writing until you try. Plus, you don't have to limit yourself to just one type of writing.

4. **Try something new**—if your story isn't working, try something new. A different point of view, style, genre, or even a new prompt if the one you're working on isn't working!

5. **Have FUN!** - Did I mention have fun? Whether you

are writing something silly or serious, creating a story is fun, so enjoy it.

6. **Write as long or as short as you like**—If you only have a few minutes, then you can write something short. It doesn't matter if you don't finish a story or piece of writing in a sitting, or at all.

7. **First drafts are meant to be crappy***—this is something many people don't realise, it's no issue if your first draft is not perfect. Everything can be fixed up in the editing process.

8. **You don't have to finish**—if you're writing for fun, and you don't finish your story, that's okay. You can always come back and finish it another time.

9. **Have FUN!** - I may have mentioned this before… have fun writing your story, poem, or whatever else you're writing.

* Crappy = flawed, imperfect, incomplete, not up to scratch, unsatisfactory

Tips on how to use Writing Prompts

1. **Read the prompt carefully**— What is it asking you to do?

2. **Think outside the box**— Is there a way you can use the prompt in a fun or unusual way?

3. **Use the prompt more than once**— If you have more than one idea, then write them down. You can use a prompt in many different ways.

4. **Just write**— Don't worry about titles, spelling, grammar, or anything else, just write. This is a first draft. Underline any words you're not sure about spelling and you can come back to them later. Everything can be fixed up in the editing process.

5. **Read over what you've written**— When you've done, read over what you've written and fix up any obvious errors. Then you can have fun editing your story to share (if you want to).

Writing Prompts

1

A teddy bear sits next to your bed. Write about the adventures it gets up to when the lights go out.

2

Write a story that solves the mystery of what happens to the odd socks.

3

Write about a superhero with unimpressive superpowers.

4

Write about a family holiday, from the point of view of the family pet.

5

Write a story about the worst birthday present ever received.

6

Write a letter from the Tooth Fairy explaining why they are late.

7

Pick a book at random.

Use the title of that book to write a story.

8

Write a story about the unusual monster that lives under your bed.

9

Write a love letter or poem to your favourite childhood toy.

10

Write a day in the life of a couch, from the point of view of the couch.

11

Write a sad story about the day you have to say goodbye to your favourite jumper.

12

Rewrite a fairy tale from the point of view of the villain.

13

Write a story with the following first line:

For most people, 13 is an unlucky number, but for me, it's the number 9.

14

Write a story about a person who wins a certificate, trophy, or other prize every day for a month.

15

Write a completely made-up history of Mother's Day, Father's Day or another non-religious day of observation.

16

Write the life story of a Grand Piano.

17

You have a magic lunchbox that always serves up the most amazing food. Write a story about the day the magic doesn't work as it should.

18

After going back in time, you discover that everything we thought we knew about dinosaurs was wrong.
Write a story about what you discover and how you go about setting the record straight.

19

So many people say no one ever remembers the person who comes second in a competition. Write a story about the person or team that everyone remembers who comes second.

20

Write a story about the person who bought a flower instead of flour by accident!

21

Write a story about the being who decides what the weather will be on any given day.

22

All superheroes and super villains need a hideout.

Write a Real Estate advertisement for a secret hideout that would be perfect for either of them.

23

Write a story about the day a dragon comes to dinner.

24

You look in the mirror, and the face looking back is not your face.

Write a story about who is in the mirror and what happens next.

25

You are staying in an old hotel and decide to go exploring. Write a story about what you discover.

26

Write a story about an everyday activity, such as washing the dishes, that has been turned into a competitive sport.

27

Write a story using the following random words:
Budgie, Coffee, Potato, Remote, Tree.

28

Write a story about a stereotypical pirate with an unusual or unlikely hobby.

29

Write a story about what happens when your muse goes on holiday – from the point of view of your muse.

30

Just for fun, you decide to dial your own phone number to see what will happen.

Someone answers the phone!

Who is it, and what happens?

31

You are an extra on a TV show, only to find out that the show is real! What happens and how do you back to your regular life?

32

Write a story and this is the last line: And that is why our car can drive on water.

33

You wake up in a world that doesn't know the colour blue. What has happened and how do you get things right again?

34

Write a story featuring too many lemons.

35

Write a story about an unexpected or unusual family tradition.

36

You invent a new kind of chocolate.

Write a story about your invention.

37

There is a secret 'parent manual' that is full of rules parents just seem to know.

Write a page from that manual.

36

You invent a new kind of chocolate.

Write a story about your invention.

37

There is a secret 'parent manual' that is full of rules parents just seem to know.

Write a page from that manual.

38

Write a story about the workers who must clean up after a superhero defeats the villain.

39

Pick a random piece of technology. You time travel to the year 1900. Explain that piece of technology to someone.

40

Write a diary entry by one of Santa's elves, on the date you are doing this exercise.

41

Write a story about the perfect cup of tea.

42

Blow something up!

(in a story, not in real life…)

43

Write a story featuring the following flowers:

Lily, Rose, Peony, Gerbera, Daffodil.

44

There is an impending disaster on Earth and, to survive, humans must reach out to aliens for help. Write a story about what happens.

45

Write a story about the day the superheroes sidekick saves the day.

46

Write a story about an unconventional princess.

47

Digging in your back yard, you discover an old treasure chest. When you open it, the contents are not what you expected. Write a story about what is inside.

48

One year, you develop the ability to hibernate over winter! Write a story about your hibernation and what it's like waking up again.

49

Often chicken soup is given to someone when they're unwell and is considered a comfort food. Write a story about an unusual comfort food.

50

You decide to attend a local bootcamp, however, when you arrive, you discover it's not quite what you expected. Write a story about your unconventional boot camp.

51

You are walking along the beach, and you find a bottle with a message inside.
What does the message say?
Write a story about the message in the bottle.

52

Write a story about a week where the days of the week are out of order. Instead of Monday, Tuesday, Wednesday, Thursday, Friday, the week may go Wednesday, Tuesday, Saturday, Friday, etc.

Conclusion

I hope you've had fun with these writing prompts and enjoyed crafting stories with them.

One fantastic thing about writing prompts is that you can use them more than once and come out with an entirely different story.

If you do want to use the prompt again and aren't quite sure what to do, try writing from a different point of view, or a different style or genre than you did last time.

Try it and see what happens.

You can use these prompts over and over to have fun with your imagination.

Happy Writing,

Melissa Gijsbers.

Author Bio

Melissa Gijsbers is an author and booklover. She started working with young writers in 2013 at the Monash Public Library and has been inspiring them to write by providing them with crazy writing prompts ever since!

She currently lives in the Latrobe Valley in Victoria, Australia and spends quite a bit of time coming up with fun writing ideas for stories, as well as writing more books herself.

You can find out more about Melissa on her website— www.melissagijsbers.com

Acknowledgements

I'd like to acknowledge all the young writers I have had the pleasure of working with, both in person and virtual workshops. They inspire me to come up with fun writing activities and we share in the joy of creating stories together.

To all my cheerleaders, including business mentors and members of various Facebook groups, who have encouraged me to put this second book of writing prompts together.

Want More?

If you want more writing prompts, be sure to check out *Genie In My Drink Bottle and Other Fun Writing Prompts*, available from Amazon and melissagijsbers.com

Great Odd Sock Mystery

Odd socks going missing!
Your muse goes on holiday!
You discover a chest with unexpected tresure!
Melissa Gijsbers has compiled 52 writing prompts from the hundreds she's used over a decade of working with young writers to use to inspire their stories, poems, or any other form of writing.